HIS
NAME

Be Still Ministries
Alpharetta, GA, USA
bestillministries.net

His Name | Our Hope in Grief

Copyright © 2022 Be Still Ministries

ISBN#
Print: 978-1-7361982-2-3
Kindle: 978-1-7361982-1-6
Library of Congress Cataloging-in-Publication Data has been applied for.

Stock or custom editions of this title may be purchased in bulk for educational, business, ministry, fundraising, or sales promotional use. For more information please email hello@bestillministries.net

Edited by Brit Eaton.
Interior Design by RGSGroup.media
Cover design by Chel Kissler
Printed in the United States of America

ENDORSEMENTS

You just picked up a book comprised of pages *filled with hope*. Jesus intimately refers to God as His Father and invites us to do the same. As you read stories of earthly heartbreak, lean in to the names that represent and reveal His person. And learn how deep, healing, and unchanging His love is for you.

Sandra and Andy Stanley
North Point Ministries

Penned from hard-fought hope, Rachel Faulkner Brown and her team of widows and friends masterfully journey us through how the names of God hold us through the hard times and teach us how to love and cling to Jesus through it all. Maybe you're picking up this book because you've been through some of the most heart-shattering days on Earth. Maybe you've lost a spouse, or know someone who has. *His Name* will encourage and remind you that God is always near and always working—even when you can't see a thing.

Shelley Giglio
Co-founder of Passion Conferences and
Passion City Church

Knowing God by name is the gateway to His heart! This is a beautiful resource for anyone who needs to be reminded of all the beautiful facets of the matchless heart of God, and to not forget all His benefits!

Christy Nockels
Worship leader, songwriter, and author of
The Life You Long For: Learning to Live from a Heart of Rest

We have based our counseling practice at Daystar around the idea that God redeems our stories—every single hurt and heartache. Rachel Faulkner Brown and the wise women who have contributed their words and their hearts to this book are living reminders of that redemption. They are walking out His story through theirs. They are pointing us all toward what it looks like to continue to not only live after loss but also to find hope in *His Name*.

Sissy Goff, LPC-MHSP, David Thomas, LMSW,
& Melissa Trevathan, MRE
Counselors, authors, speakers
daystar Counseling Ministries

Even for those who dearly love and walk with the Lord, it is impossible for us to scratch the surface of understanding His character, His attributes, and ultimately His mercy and might in full. When we learn about, meditate on, and pray all the unique names that He calls Himself, we get a glimpse behind the curtain. We gain access as His children to deeper parts of His heart. We learn to love Him and lean on Him in the most life-sustaining ways.

Mattie Jackson Selecman
Widow, author of *Lemons on Friday*

TABLE OF CONTENTS

INTRODUCTION

Years ago, our Never Alone Widows team gathered around the table for a pre-retreat lunch and shared a beautiful idea. It's the book you're holding in your hands—a precious collection of the stories and scriptures that changed us forever in our own seasons of grief and loss.

I'll never forget us calling on the names of the Lord and speaking this 30-day devotional into existence. Even then, we knew it would change the heart, life, and story of every widow who found her way through its pages. This devotional is your opportunity to re-write your own grief narrative as a story of hope, co-created with the heart of God.

God's promises to us as widows never change.
His Word will never return void and **His Name** is the strong and mighty tower we can always run to.

I believe grief is the most holy of all work. When you lean toward the One, He not only leans back, but He leans in, He whispers new mercies, and He overdelivers on His promises that can't be undone by your circumstances. I've been widowed twice and therefore cling tightly to every one of these truths.

God is able—and willing—to show up *exactly* how you need Him to on your healing journey. He will meet you where you are in your grief as "Jehovah Rapha" (Your Healer), "Jehovah Jireh" (Your Provider), or "Yahweh" (Your Lord). It's my prayer that you encounter Him fresh and new in and through one of His many powerful names.

Keep in mind as you go, the names you learn, the stories you read, the scriptures you reference, and even the journal entries you write may not make sense right away. That's okay Processing grief is exactly what it sounds like: a *process*. Rest assured that one day you will look back on this precious collection of stories (including your own!) as a transformational turning point on your own journey toward hope Himself.

No matter where you are on your grief journey, God is there, grieving with you, even when it feels like He's not. You've never been alone. And, sweet friend, you never will be.

Over the next 30 days, I pray you feel surrounded in His presence as His Word comes alive in you. I pray you add new facets of His name and character to your arsenal of healing. And I pray you "grow stronger and stronger with every step forward" (Psalm 84:7 TPT) in the powerful name of Jesus. This is indeed your inheritance.

Yours in hope and healing,

Rachel

Rachel Faulkner Brown
Executive Director, Be Still Ministries

"Faith means believing in advance what will only make sense in reverse."

PHILIP YANCEY

JEHOVAH SHAMMAH
THE LORD IS THERE

COURTNEY PRAY DUKE, WIDOW

"I took you from the ends of the earth, from its farthest corners I called you. I said, 'You are my servant'; I have chosen you and have not rejected you. So do not fear, for I am with you; do not be dismayed, for I am your God. I will strengthen you and help you; I will uphold you with my righteous right hand." Isaiah 41:9-10 (NIV)

God is not the least bit surprised by your circumstances. Even in this very moment, He feels your intense pain and loneliness and intimately understands the ache of your soul.

In the early weeks and months after losing my husband to a tragic accident and being left to raise three young children by myself, I felt absolutely suffocated. I found so much strength in taking God's Word and speaking His promises out loud, even when I didn't believe it or feel like it. Sometimes hearing yourself speak His Word back to Him is not only powerful but also productive as it helps you take courageous steps forward when you feel stuck.

In the dark of night, I would literally cling to the scripture above in Isaiah. On days when I didn't know what to do or where to go, God's Word became my sustenance, giving me life and breath in the very bottom of the valley.

Not only is God not surprised by the road you're walking today, but He is also right there with you. Not far off, uninterested, and passively standing by—but actively sitting right in the middle of your pain and suffering with you.

The scripture above says that Almighty God has called you by name and chosen you as His very own. Fear has to bow down, in the name of Jesus. Why? Because God is with you. His power and purposes for your life are greater than anything the enemy wants to throw at you. Jehovah Shammah is there, and He promises to never leave you or forsake you. What a promise to take hold of in the dark of night!

Friend, God hasn't abandoned you, leaving you in the ruins. There will be restoration! He will be faithful to lead you all the way through and out of this season, one trusting step at a time. The Lord makes rivers flow out of barren places and puts lush greenery in the desert so that everyone will know that God alone has done it (see Isaiah 41). When Jehovah Shammah steps on the scene, everything changes. The Lord is there.

JOURNAL

Reflect on your life up to your current situation. Where has God been in the past, and where might He be now, even if you can't see Him?

_____

_____

_____

_____

_____

_____

_____

_____

_____

_____

_____

_____

_____

_____

EL ROI
THE LORD WHO SEES

BRITTANY PRICE BROOKER, WIDOW

"You are [El Roi] a God of seeing. Truly, here I have seen Him who looks after me." Genesis 16:13 (NKJV)

After a long day of trying to survive being a single mom—facing every grief trigger and holding the heartache of those around me—I crawled into bed one night and let it all out. In the dark of night, I cried out to God with my questions.

Do You see my heart right now?
Do You see this pain?
Do You see what my babies are going through?

I felt the deep, peaceful presence of El Roi: God Who Sees. And I wasn't the first.

In Genesis, we find the story of Hagar, a woman trying to flee from an incredibly uncomfortable life. As she tries to escape the title and pain she doesn't want, the Lord speaks to her. He calls her by name—not by a title someone else gave her.

God pursues her. The God Who Sees was willing to come after her in the wilderness and meet her in her pain. Hagar's famous response in the scripture above says it all—she realizes she was seen, precious, and valuable in the eyes of God.

Sweet sister, you may be in the wilderness. You may be on the run from your pain, from the title of "widow" that you never wanted. You may be on the run from having to look and act strong, fearing nobody really sees you and your pain. You may be running from having to muster all your strength to simply survive.

Take heart! El Roi sees you and is looking after you, even in the dark of night.

In the days when the pain feels like it might kill you, He is there. He not only sees you, but He cares for you and is looking out for you and your family.

JOURNAL

When was the last time you felt like God really saw you? How does it make you feel to know He sees you right now?

3

JEHOVAH SHALOM
THE LORD IS PEACE

PAIGE KNUDSEN, WIDOW

*"The Lord is my shepherd; I shall not want. He maketh me to lie down in green pastures: he leadeth me beside the still waters."
Psalm 23:1-2 (KJV)*

One of my most impactful memories is growing up in a home where I saw my mom spend time with Jesus. We lived in a two-story traditional house complete with a den, living room, dining room, and kitchen on the first floor, like many homes built in the 1970s. In my mind's eye, each room held memories of a joy-filled childhood. But the living room? Well, *that's* the room where Mom spent so much time at the feet of Jesus.

I'd come downstairs each morning to find her with her well-worn Bible, her journals, a hymnal, and her cassette tape player. She scribbled on notecards to encourage younger ones in the faith. She spent time in prayer. She spent time in worship. She spent time getting to know her heavenly Father, chasing after the heart of Jesus, and welcoming the Spirit to invade every part of her life. And it wasn't just in the morning. I could find her there in the living room at any time of day.

Several years ago, a publishing company gifted me with their newly released *Names of God Bible*. I knew my mom would absolutely love it, so I quickly gifted it to her—right before her health situation became extremely complicated. Her mental and physical health took a turn for the worse, and she entered short-term nursing care.

Even now, in the throes of a global pandemic, our only form of communication with Mom is through the window to her room. Each time I visit her, I catch a glimpse of her bedside table where a large water cup, colored pencils, and the *Names of God Bible* naturally sit. On a recent visit, she seemed to have a little more clarity than usual. She told me she was reading about Jehovah Shalom: The Lord Is Peace.

Tears flowed. Did she forget about the virus? Or that nursing homes are seemingly the most susceptible? Did she forget her age and that she can't walk on her own?

I knew the Spirit of the Lord, the Lord of Peace, was actually right there with us, ministering His peace to us both. My mom was still teaching me about the character and nature of God, which gives us peace in the midst of the storm. In the middle of unknown and tragic circumstances, when my heart is breaking, He covers my mind with His peace. Even as my mom's mind and body drift away, He gives her peaceful thoughts because she knows Him. She knows His voice and character because she drew near to Him every day for so many years.

I don't understand why it has to be this way. I have no idea what her future holds. But I know God is drawing near to my mom. He has given me the eyes to see it. I see the evidence of His Spirit and character wash over her as evidence of her faith.

On that particular visit, the nurse left the window cracked open for me. I played her a scripture reading of Psalm 23 on my phone, as loud as possible, through that one-inch crack. The narrator's beautiful African accent, combined with the images of green pastures, quiet waters, and the peaceful places our Shepherd of Peace gives us as we walk through the valley, will stay with me forever. It was a beautifully raw, tender, full-circle moment for me. I once again witnessed my mom at the feet of her heavenly Father, Jehovah Shalom.

JOURNAL

In what ways has God revealed Himself as Jehovah Shalom, God of Peace, to you? How can you tap into His peace that passes understanding today?

_____

_____

_____

_____

_____

_____

_____

_____

_____

_____

_____

_____

_____

_____

4

JEHOVAH JIREH
THE LORD WILL PROVIDE

MADI KNUDSEN, WIDOW DAUGHTER

"Abraham looked up and there in a thicket he saw a ram caught by its horns. He went over and took the ram and sacrificed it as a burnt offering instead of his son. So Abraham called that place The Lord Will Provide. And to this day it is said, 'On the mountain of the Lord it will be provided.'" Genesis 22:13-14 (NIV)

I don't know about you, but when I read my Bible, a movie starts playing out in my head. The characters change often; sometimes it's Chris Pine as Jesus, and sometimes it's one of the Veggie Tales. Along with each movie reel comes my own internal narrative.

One day as I was reading in Genesis, I came across the story of Abraham and his son Isaac. Abraham (played by Michael

Landon in this particular reel) and Isaac (played by Linwood Boomer—Adam from *Little House on the Prairie*) are headed up the mountain where Abraham is about to sacrifice his son in obedience to God.

My thoughts swirled as I questioned what God was asking of Abraham. *What's happening, God? You want him to sacrifice his beautiful blessing?* Abraham's faith in that moment was incredible. I can't imagine what he was feeling as he stood over Isaac with a knife in his hand, ready to strike. But God! God stops him and provides a little ram for the sacrifice instead.

God always provides. When I read the Bible, I'm always quick to see it. But in my own life, I admit I struggle to believe He will.

Do I trust Him to provide for the meals I need this week?
Do I trust Him to provide the finances for my house?
Do I trust Him to provide for my future?

Or do I hold everything close to my chest in fear as I try to keep all the pieces from falling?

How quickly I forget: the God who provided the ram in the thicket for Abraham is the *same* God who provided us all with the perfect sacrifice of Jesus, the Lamb of God. This is the same God who will provide for me. He is Jehovah Jireh. His provision doesn't always come the way I think it should or when I think I need it most. But it's always perfect.

I don't want to wait until the end of my life's movie reel to say God provided. In the messy middle of my story, I proclaim with every fiber of my being: *Jehovah Jireh, my God, has provided!*

JOURNAL

In what ways has God provided for you and your family in the past? In what ways do you need to trust Him to provide for you now and into the future?

_____

_____

_____

_____

_____

_____

_____

_____

_____

_____

_____

_____

_____

YAHWEH
I Am Who I Am

RACHEL FAULKNER BROWN, MILITARY WIDOW

"Restore our fortunes, Lord, like streams in the Negev. Those who sow with tears will reap with songs of joy. Those who go out weeping, carrying seed to sow, will return with songs of joy, carrying sheaves with them." Psalm 126:4-6 (NIV)

A few years ago, my life was changed with a simple fact found in brain science. I remember hearing the words that felt so sticky I knew I would never forget them:

"Rachel, scientifically, you can only hold a strong emotion for 90 seconds."

Ummmm, what?!
This grief isn't going to kill me?
Because right now it feels like it's going to kill me!

Chances are, you know that feeling. Being so broken down and crying so hard that your eyes and heart are literally sore. Yeah, that kind of 90 seconds. Brain researcher Jill Bolte Taylor wrote a book called *A Brain Scientist's Personal Journey* on this very thought. According to Taylor, when we understand that it takes 90 seconds for our systems to fully process emotions, we can acknowledge them and let them pass naturally. But when we fight the emotion, we make it worse by perpetuating the problem. This gives the emotion power over us and keeps us stuck.[1]

When we have awareness that all emotions initially last for 90 seconds, we can allow them to ripple through us, causing a wave without any resistance. We can let them go without causing further reaction. If we allow emotions to pass through us naturally, we can take an honest look at what story we might have attached to the emotion to heighten its effects and trigger us to respond.

Psalm 126 is the well of all wells for the broken. It has given me life, it has powered me into the hard, and it has allowed me to *rejoice* in the tears that have given new birth to joy.

Yahweh, do it again! Let your name—the I AM—partner with us in the grief and in the joy. You created us to hold emotion and release it. You created us to experience the wave and then surrender to the peace. May it be so in us, Jesus.

21

JOURNAL

What emotions have you partnered with that have not been released and sown back into the ground? What words stood out to you in the scripture above, and why?

_____

_____

_____

_____

_____

_____

_____

_____

_____

_____

_____

_____

_____

_____

6

JEHOVAH JIREH
THE LORD WILL PROVIDE

GINGER GILBERT RAVELLA, MILITARY WIDOW

"So Abraham called the name of that place, 'The Lord will provide'; as it is said to this day, 'On the mount of the Lord it shall be provided.'" Genesis 22:14 (ESV)

Even as I type this, I hear familiar lyrics from a childhood song: "Jehovah Jireh, my Provider, His Grace is sufficient for me." Growing older and facing the hard of life, I had to trust that these words were more than just a catchy tune. Desperate to know how and when God would provide, the question arose in my heart: *In the dark of night, would these words really ring true?*

Abraham must have wondered the same thing as he walked the hill, carrying firewood and holding his son Isaac's hand. God had asked him to do the unthinkable: sacrifice his beloved child. The Bible doesn't tell us much about what was going through Abraham's head, or Isaac's for that matter. However, we know from Hebrews that Abraham knew God had promised him a legacy and that He could raise the dead. He knew that even if the knife took his son's life, God would still make a way.

After my husband's sudden and tragic death, I felt the same— slain but looking to the Way Maker for a resurrection. I believe the Lord allowed what was most precious to me to be taken away, the earthly security and future in which I'd placed my hope, so that I would stand on the unshakable knowledge that no matter what, He *will provide.*

Man's extremity is God's opportunity. It's in the extremes, the places we fear most to go, that we find our own ram in the thicket—the way *out* or the way *through.*

Do you question the sacrifice God has asked you to make? I know I did. Unlike any other time in your life, the loss of your spouse is *the time* the Lord will ask you to remember who He is. He's asking you to remember His own Son whom He sacrificed for you (and your children and your children's children!).

Your legacy is secure. Your hope isn't lost. You are His lamb and He is your ram.

JOURNAL

What scary and/or difficult things has God asked you to do? In what ways has He been willing to make a way out or a way through for you?

_____

_____

_____

_____

_____

_____

_____

_____

_____

_____

_____

_____

_____

_____

IMMANUEL
GOD With Us

BELLA RAVELLA, WIDOW, DAUGHTER

"Therefore the Lord himself will give you a sign. Behold, the virgin shall conceive and bear a son, and shall call his name Immanuel." Isaiah 7:14 (ESV)

To anyone observing my life, last December looked cheery. I was attending holiday parties, wrapping Christmas gifts, and loving extra big on family and friends. Simply put, that month appeared to be exactly as it should: a sweet mix of both celebration and rest. But truthfully, my heart never felt more the opposite.

In early December, a young man from my Bible study was tragically injured in a drive-by shooting. Following a week of hospital gatherings and intense prayer, he went to be with Jesus. Though the two of us weren't close, I was brokenhearted along with the rest of our close-knit community.

Unexpectedly, that loss triggered a more familiar one. I found myself suddenly grieving anew for the loss of my dad. Although he went to heaven in 2006, I felt his absence so heavily in the system shock of that month. Through that season of fresh pain, I was fully awakened to God as Immanuel. Without the pain, I could not fully understand the hope found in knowing our heavenly Father as the One who truly dwells with us.

Loss and fear open our hearts to a deep knowledge of God like nothing else can. Our painful experiences close the imaginary gap that we are so convinced exists between us and the Father. In Isaiah 7, God speaks through the prophet to King Ahaz, a leader wracked with fear about Judah's looming destruction. God challenges him to release long-held unfaithfulness and instead trust in deliverance. In the scripture above, Isaiah promises Ahaz a miraculous sign that will be a sign for the long-expected Messiah—Jesus—God in the flesh.

The promise of "God With Us" was fashioned into the name Immanuel for the very first time in this prophecy. But the name reaches far beyond the Old Testament. Matthew repeats the name when he writes of the angel appearing to Joseph. Mary, Joseph's virgin bride-to-be, would conceive a son who would be called Immanuel (see Matthew 1:18-22). Jesus was the deliverance, the ultimate fulfillment of God's promise. He was Immanuel, the One who dwells with us.

In my seeking, I came to understand the full truth: We are post Jesus' time on Earth, post His conception, and post His crucifixion. But that does not mean we are on our own. We still walk daily in His *commission* (see Matthew 28:16-20).

In the same breath that Jesus commands us to go and make disciples of all nations, baptizing and teaching, He reminds us that we are not to walk it alone. He firmly declares, "And surely I am with you always, to the very end of the age" (v. 20 NIV). God's promise extends from the beginning of creation in Genesis until His coming, physical reign in Revelation!

Embrace these truths found in scripture today with the knowledge that our God is indeed Immanuel, not just during Christmas, hymn-sings, and difficult seasons. Immanuel is with you in every moment.

JOURNAL

Do you believe God is with you? How can you step into that place of intimacy in your current sorrow and in the joy to come?

_____

_____

_____

_____

_____

_____

_____

_____

_____

_____

_____

_____

_____

BRIDEGROOM
GOD OF UNCONDITIONAL LOVE

KAREN McADAMS, PRAYER TEAM

"You are altogether beautiful, my darling; there is no flaw in you." Song of Solomon 4:7 (NIV)

By the time I was 25 years old, I was tired of trying: trying to be perfect, trying to find love, trying to be enough for everyone else. Engaged twice, I made it as far as 10 days away from the altar on my second go. I felt used, rejected, dirty, and unworthy of love. I felt especially unworthy of wearing that white dress. I believed the lie that I was not enough, which had been communicated to me by every guy I had ever known.

To be fair, my heart had believed that message for so long that it didn't take a failed engagement to solidify it. At the tender age of eight, my innocence was stolen and my ears were opened to a new voice: the voice of shame. That voice became the dominant voice in my life for decades to follow.

Until Jesus—my Bridegroom.

By age 30, I finally made it down the aisle in a rented wedding dress—at the very beginning of my journey to Jesus. I was doubling down in all of my "trying," but I couldn't shake the feeling that I would never measure up. I was sure I would always be under God's certain-to-be-disappointed gaze. Boy, did I have Him all wrong.

One night, in quiet desperation, I did the Bible "trick."

Jesus, will You please open the Bible to whatever You want me to read?

The book fell open to the Song of Solomon. By the time I had finished reading the text, I was confident this book should *not* be in the Bible! But the next day, the strangest thing happened. The woman checking my son into the church daycare asked if I would wear my wedding dress during a pageant at the upcoming women's conference. The conference theme was the Song of Solomon! I could hardly believe my ears.

In the moments that followed, the shackles began to break off my wounded soul as she shared that the story told in the

Song of Solomon revealed Jesus as my Bridegroom and me as His "beautiful, spotless bride." Those three words were all it took to crack the code on the shame I was carrying. Three words undid a lifetime of self-hatred and opened the door to unconditional *love.*

Have you ever felt less-than? Unworthy? Not enough?

Remind yourself today of these three words: *Beautiful. Spotless. Bride!*

Father God Himself chose *you* for His Son—your heavenly Bridegroom.

JOURNAL

How does it make you feel to know Jesus is your heavenly Bridegroom—and that no matter your story, you are His beautiful, spotless bride?

_____

_____

_____

_____

_____

_____

_____

_____

_____

_____

_____

_____

_____

9

JEHOVAH JIREH
THE LORD WILL PROVIDE

VIRGINIA SCHROEDER, PRAYER TEAM

"And my God will meet all your needs according to the riches of his glory in Christ Jesus." Philippians 4:19 (NIV)

Wanting a child so badly, I battled through years of infertility. Endometriosis was the enemy in my fight.

After a series of tests, pharmacological protocols, and failed surgeries, adoption was our next option for having a family. One year later, my husband and I adopted a beautiful baby boy. We were filled with joy!

However, the joy didn't last long. After having our son in our home for one week, his birth mother changed her mind and he was taken away. The grief overwhelmed me. I was filled with hopelessness in the reality of devastating loss.

But God.

Two days later, my sister led me to Christ.

Three weeks later, I held my first daughter in my arms.

Throughout the years, I have heard God whisper:

I am for you and not against you. In the trials of your life, I am Jehovah Jireh.

He tells me to lay down my Isaacs on the altar. And when I do, He always makes provision. I worship Jehovah Jireh in obedience, knowing that whatever I need, He will provide. He has shown Himself faithful, time and time again.

Close your eyes and see yourself with Jesus in your favorite place. Allow hope to come alive in His presence. Know that God will come through for you. Release the reins of your life—your Isaacs—into His hands.

JOURNAL

In what unexpected ways have you experienced God revealing Himself as provider? What needs were met, and how? Be honest with your feelings and allow the Holy Spirit to flood you with His presence as you write.

10

I AM
CREATOR GOD

JORDIN EARLY, COUNSELOR

"God said to Moses, 'I AM WHO I AM. This is what you are to say to the Israelites: I AM has sent me to you.'" Exodus 3:14 (NIV)

Many of the names of God are specific to His characteristics: Comforter, Most High, Everlasting. However, one of His names is open-ended: Creator. He can be all things in all seasons of life.

We learn about our Father, the Creator, in the earliest parts of the Old Testament. For nearly 400 years after the fall of Adam and Eve, the children of Israel assumed that their God was either AWOL or on vacation—or maybe even dead. The Hebrew people, who were Abraham's descendants, found themselves in bondage in a foreign land. God had made a promise to Abraham that his descendants would be a mighty nation and possess the land of Canaan. But the reality was, they were enslaved in Egypt.

How could this be? God had assured them that He would be their God and that He would never leave them—that they were His chosen children. Such lavish promises seem like a cruel joke when you're in chains and God hasn't been heard from for centuries.

I wonder if their thoughts echoed ours.

If God is real, where is He when I need Him?

Where is He when I am in pain?

Maybe I misunderstood His promises—or maybe they weren't promises at all?

Moses wrestled with doubts. Living in exile in Midian, he needed a burning bush to be reminded of God's promises. God told him to go back to Egypt and lead His people to freedom. When Moses asked who he should say sent him, God answered simply, "I AM" (Exodus 3:14).

I AM—the meaning is powerful. It's timeless and constant, never changing in a constantly changing world. I AM always is. Where chaos occurs, I AM is secure. Where there is hurt,

I AM is hope. Where pain is prevalent, I AM is a comforter. Where there is loneliness, I AM is a friend. When attacked, I AM is the defender. When broken, I AM is the healer. When feeling unloved, I AM is love. Whatever you need I AM to be, He is! I AM is always enough.

The Israelites may not have been familiar with God, but He was familiar with them. I AM knew who they were! He knew they would struggle to believe in a God they could not see. He knew they would be fickle and faithless and that they would need constant rescue from the consequences of their own foolish choices. And yet He still set His affection upon them.

I AM, I believe You are the one true God. You are near and You never change. Even though I don't completely understand, I believe You will never fail me. Help me to rely on Your presence, God, and to trust in Your constant faithfulness. Amen.

JOURNAL

Write down five words that describe you. Which of your attributes best reflects the heart of God? If you could be known for one characteristic, what would it be, and why?

_____

_____

_____

_____

_____

_____

_____

_____

_____

_____

_____

_____

_____

_____

PEACE
GOD OF ALL PEACE

ALLISON BARTON PETERS, WIDOW

"You keep him in perfect peace whose mind is stayed on you, because he trusts in you." Isaiah 26:3 (ESV)

Oddly enough, the times in my life that are marked by the greatest turmoil, loss, and need for total dependence on Jesus have also been the times when I have felt the most peace.

According to Webster's Dictionary, "peace" means "freedom from disturbance" or "tranquility." I now recognize that in those moments of turmoil and loss, the Holy Spirit was freeing me from either the disturbance and chaos deep within myself or from that which surrounded me. He was focusing my heart on the foundation of hope and security that I have in Jesus.

In my life, peace has come after leaving a relationship that was causing discord and unrest. Hope was confirmed and peace instilled when as a family, we prayed together and ushered my dad's soul into the gates of heaven after an eight-month battle with cancer. I rested in abounding peace as I chose to believe God's promise to care for and comfort my broken heart after I experienced a miscarriage where questions went unanswered and dreams of another child disappeared.

I intimately recognized a familiar yet unexplainable calm as I stood in the ER, watching the hustle and desperation of staff as they tried to revive my 35-year-old husband, only to deliver the gut-wrenching news that he was gone. Amidst the shock and trauma, there was peace—even though I knew I would never see him again this side of heaven.

Peace is a compass. It's a gift the Holy Spirit gives us as believers. It's often unexplainable yet recognized and acknowledged as it brings harmony and security. When reflecting on peace and what it's meant to me over the years, the Holy Spirit laid upon my heart an old hymn called *It Is Well.*

The significance of the hymn is not lost on me. Horatio Spafford, who penned its words, did so shortly after he lost his wife and four daughters in a shipwreck. His lyrics focus less on what was lost and more on where hope can be found. What a great reminder that in the midst of being shattered by the loss of his family, his heart still turned to the faithfulness of God.

The peace of the Lord is present in the pain—*Your* pain—and His peace is always greater!

When peace like a river attendeth my way,
When sorrows like sea billows roll;
Whatever my lot,
Thou hast taught me to say,
"It is well, it is well with my soul!"

JOURNAL

When have you experienced the peace that passes understanding? What things tend to threaten that peace in your life, and why?

_____

_____

_____

_____

_____

_____

_____

_____

_____

_____

_____

_____

_____

_____

_____

12

JEHOVAH JIREH
The LORD Will Provide

Molly Moody Davidson, Worship Team

"Command those who are rich in this present world not to be arrogant nor to put their hope in wealth, which is so uncertain, but to put their hope in God, who richly provides us with everything for our enjoyment. Command them to do good, to be rich in good deeds, and to be generous and willing to share. In this way they will lay up treasure for themselves as a firm foundation for the coming age, so that they may take hold of the life that is truly life." 1 Timothy 6:17-19 (NIV)

"I'm thirty-six and still single." That's a story that I never thought would be mine. Don't get me wrong. I never saw myself as married and pregnant at twenty-two, but I didn't think that I'd be over halfway into my thirties and still doing life by myself.

So, what's a girl to do when she is out on her own for all these years? She rolls up her sleeves and she gets it done. In my mind, I knew that God was my provider. But somewhere in my heart, I had a hard time believing that He really would come through for me in *every* way. I was unknowingly driven by the lie that "it's up to me" to pay my bills, to find a man, and to prove myself successful.

And then along came Corona. Nothing like a global pandemic to take you to a new level of despair, right? I found myself losing 90 percent of my work after moving to a new city. I felt lost and desperate for direction. *What the heck am I gonna do? What's my place in all of this?*

Shortly after, the still, small voice of God came and whispered clearly to my heart. I was ready to hear His words in a new way.

Let Me provide for you. Better than money, let Me provide everything you need.

My initial thoughts were, *Okay, so what do I do? What do I owe You?* But I have discovered the only requirement is to *receive*—to daily, sometimes hourly, repent of the lie that "it's up to me" and simply *receive* God's provision.

My eyes have become open to all the ways that God is providing multiple blessings in my life—giving me every penny I need, but beyond that, in His lavish love, He is giving me the deep treasures of His heart.

Life has not looked like I thought it would. But with Jehovah Jireh by my side, the One "who richly provides us with everything for our enjoyment," I am learning how to believe that I will never be in want again.

JOURNAL

In what ways do you try to control your world, not trusting God to come through? Invite Him to show you how He is your true provider in every way.

_____

_____

_____

_____

_____

_____

_____

_____

_____

_____

_____

_____

_____

13

JEHOVAH RAPHA
THE LORD WHO HEALS

BROOKE TALLEY, WIDOW

"O Lord my God, I cried to you for help and you have healed me. O Lord, you have brought up my soul from Sheol; you restored me to life from among those who go down to the pit." Psalm 30:2-3 (NLT)

When we decide to walk out of the grave and into God's promises of healing and redemption, the enemy will wage war over our stories of restoration and healing. We have to choose to fight to see that the Lord is Jehovah Rapha: The Lord Who Heals.

How do we fight? Faith is a powerful weapon as we battle to see our Lord come through as Jehovah Rapha. In the scriptures, we see faith go hand in hand with physical healing.

That same faith is the foundation on which we stand when we ask God to enter in and heal our broken hearts.

The Israelites stood on the edge of the land that was promised to them. It was filled with beauty, just as they had been told. However, in addition to seeing the beauty, they also saw the obstacles before them. They became fearful of bearing more grief and spending more time in the wilderness. Would they choose to receive the gift of milk and honey before them or succumb to the pressing fear?

I can relate so much to this scene. I often battle to recognize the lies of the enemy in order to see God move as Jehovah Rapha. When we find ourselves gazing at the promised land with a cloud cover of fear, we must identify the lies and crush them before they take root. God promises deep wholeness and beauty after our wilderness wandering. His plan will never leave us in the desert.

One day, you will hear God whisper to your heart that your cast is ready to be removed and your legs are well and strong. He will ask you to take another step of faith by getting up and walking. Believe you have been made whole by the power of Jehovah Rapha: The Lord Who Heals!

"Be sober-minded; be watchful. Your adversary the devil prowls around like a roaring lion, seeking someone to devour. Resist him, firm in your faith, knowing that the same kinds of suffering are being experienced by your brotherhood throughout the world. And after you have suffered a little while, the God of all grace, who has called you to his eternal glory in Christ, will himself restore, confirm, strengthen, and establish you. To him be the dominion forever and ever, Amen" (1 Peter 5:8-11 ESV).

JOURNAL

What promises of God are you standing on? What lies are you believing? What is Jehovah Rapha asking you to step out in faith and do today?

_____

_____

_____

_____

_____

_____

_____

_____

_____

_____

_____

_____

_____

14

EL ROI
GOD WHO SEES ME

JESSICA PARKER, WIDOW

"She called the name of the LORD who spoke to her, 'You are El Roi,' for she said, 'Here I have seen the one who sees me.'" Genesis 16:13 (NHEB)

God knows what you're going through right now. He sees you, He hears your every prayer, and He catches even the smallest tear that drops from your eye. If you're feeling traumatized and broken, rest in the truth that He goes out of His way to bring restoration.

In Genesis 16, we're introduced to a hidden hero, Hagar. She's an Egyptian servant who was chosen to bear Abram's child. She had dreams and was confident. But, after being mistreated by Sarai, Abram's wife, she fled to the wilderness.

In the moment that Hagar believed there was nothing left to sustain her and she had no place of belonging, we read that she was met at a spring of water by the Angel of the Lord. There her eyes were opened to the God of hope. In her loneliness and pain, she was reminded that she was chosen for a mighty story written specifically for her. Hagar met the God of all comfort when she least expected it, and in that moment, she realized she was seen and heard.

Consequently, she gave God the name El Roi, which quite literally means "He sees."

I can identify with Hagar and maybe you can, too. Maybe you're feeling abandoned and traumatized like she was. Friends, this is a timeless reminder for us today: nothing escapes El Roi's notice. Our God is a God of seeing. His plan isn't easy or painless, but He promises to meet us in it and walk us through it.

Just like Hagar, God encounters us in the places we least expect. He's always pursuing us and we always have His full attention.

Grab ahold of the promises God has for you and offer Jesus your full surrender. If your dreams have been shattered, they will be restored. You will experience His redemption. He only has the best intentions for you. What you consider possible is far too limited for the God of the universe. His Word says He will keep you in perfect peace when your mind is fixed on Him (see Isaiah 26:3).

Jesus wants to meet with you and sit with you in your pain. Let Him in and you will experience true healing. I encourage you to saturate yourself in His Word and let Him reveal Himself and His plan to you. Allow Him to be the God of All Hope, the God of All Comfort, who sees you. Jesus, give us a greater awareness of Your nearness!

JOURNAL

What areas of your life do you need to surrender as you embrace God's plan?

_____

_____

_____

_____

_____

_____

_____

_____

_____

_____

_____

_____

_____

YAHWEH
GOD OF JACOB AND ISRAEL

KARA McCLOUD, WIDOW

"See what kind of love the Father has given to us, that we should be called children of God; and so we are." 1 John 3:1 (ESV)

After my husband of 13 years suddenly died of a heart condition, I attended a group support program. One of the goals of the grief journey was to establish a new identity after loss.

Honestly, this hurt. I was so proud of my identity in the life I had with Stephen. We had been best friends for more than half our lives and he was the only life I knew. I did not want a new identity.

Shortly after that group session, God gave me the following scripture out of Isaiah at a church retreat.

"But now, O Jacob, listen to the LORD who created you. O Israel, the one who formed you says, 'Do not be afraid, for I have ransomed you. I have called you by name; you are mine'" (Isaiah 43:1 NLT).

This was a turning point in my healing. The Lord, Yahweh, was speaking to me, His child, to redefine my identity in Him. I had been a believer since I was a young girl, but I never felt like I really "needed" God. I had all I needed in life with my family, friends, and work—so I frequently treated my Father like an afterthought.

When Stephen died, I was broken. But God's grace was abundant. In His steadfast love, God used this tremendous loss to revive my spirit in Him. My identity is now daughter, His daughter. No matter what may come in this life, I know that my identity in Christ is where I am whole.

Yahweh, the same God of Jacob and Israel, has redeemed me. He has called me by name, and I am His.

JOURNAL

What is your identity? Who does God say that you are? What do these passages mean to you?

_____

_____

_____

_____

_____

_____

_____

_____

_____

_____

_____

_____

_____

_____

16

JEHOVAH NISSI
THE LORD MY BANNER

REBECCA PARTAIN, PRAYER TEAM

"And Moses built an altar and named it 'The LORD is my Banner.'" Exodus 17:15 (NASB)

Four years ago, the most difficult season of my life came to an end. The seven years prior had been filled with one painful event after another, characterized by sickness, stroke, and death. Losing my mother to ovarian cancer was heart-wrenching, and watching my sister and brother-in-love wrestle with the after effects of his stroke was tough. However, learning that both of my daughters had individual stories of sexual abuse was the most painful and difficult experience of all. I was ill-prepared to hear or handle the words that poured from their lips as they shared their teenage experiences. As a mom, nothing could have prepared me for that kind of devastation, and I struggled to handle the full weight of their disclosure as I held in my hands the dust left from the shattered hope of the story I would have written for them. I was angry and heartbroken for the journey that my girls would now walk, and in that moment, shame and guilt became my identity.

I'll never forget the moment I pointed my finger heavenward to Abba God and declared, "I can do this better than You. You are neither faithful nor trustworthy."

At that moment, I questioned the character of God for the first time in my life. Thankfully, God neither quits nor gives up on us—even when we quit and give up on Him. Over the next two years, Abba God, in His loving and gentle way, turned His eyes and heart toward me and leaned in. He set me on a path of healing by allowing me the space to ask Him honest, hard, and vulnerable questions, a journey to really know and encounter Him. I could actually feel my dry bones come back to life (see Ezekiel 37:1-14).

In Exodus 17, the Israelites were fighting the Amalekites during their trek from Egypt to the Promised Land. The trek had been arduous for God's chosen people, and while His presence was with them day and night, they continued to question His goodness and faithfulness. The Amalekites were a group of fierce warriors whose land the Israelites had to cross in order to get to the Promised Land.

A battle broke out. Standing on a hillside nearby was Moses, Aaron, and Hur. When Moses raised his hands in the air, the Israelites would take the upper hand. But as the battle wore on, Moses grew tired. When his arms began to drop, Aaron and Hur stepped in to hold them up. Because of God's faithfulness, the nation of Israel prevailed. On that battlefield, Moses built an altar and named it Jehovah Nissi—which means "The Lord is my banner."

Throughout history, banners have been used to mark significant occasions. They hold special meaning for those who raise them but also for those who see them. When Moses built the altar and called it "The Lord Is My Banner," he was creating a place of remembrance, victory, and thanksgiving. He made a declaration that we get to share in today: The Lord is my banner and I am the Lord's.

Two years into my journey of healing, I had the privilege of going to Israel with my family. I spent time sitting in the Garden of Gethsemane reading God's Word, specifically the account of the crucifixion of Jesus. As I quietly wept at what Jesus had endured for me, I heard His gentle and quiet voice whisper within me, *I am trustworthy.*

As I tipped my chin upward, I sensed the truth of those words, words I had questioned and denied about God. I saw my precious Papa's heart for me, for my girls, for my family, and for our collective future. I knew in that moment that yes, He is trustworthy and faithful.

At our next stop, the Western Wall, I scribbled these words on a piece of paper and stuck it into a tiny crack, as is the tradition: "I will trust You for You are good."

It was there that I came to know Abba God as Jehovah Nissi like Moses did—creating a place of remembrance, celebrating my victory in Christ, and offering an expression of thanksgiving. It was there that I declared who God is, what He has done, my belief in what He will do, and that I am His dearly and deeply loved baby girl. My banner is raised—for me but also for you.

JOURNAL

Have you ever questioned God's character and goodness? In what ways can you declare His faithfulness in remembrance, victory, and thanksgiving? What does your banner say?

JEHOVAH MEKODDISHKEM
THE LORD WHO SANCTIFIES

LISA PECK, COUNSELOR

"Jesus said to her, 'I am the resurrection and the life. The one who believes in me will live, even though they die; and whoever lives by believing in me will never die. Do you believe this?'"
John 11:25-26 (NIV)

During my season of grief, I prayed and prayed to no avail for the Lord to take away my pain. Then I read *The Fire of Delayed Answers* by Bob Sorge and was undone when I learned about Jehovah Mekoddishkem: The Lord Who Sanctifies.[2]

When we cry out to God and don't readily see Him answer, the lies we believe about Him bubble to the surface. In John 11, we read of Martha and Mary's accusation of Jesus: "If you had been here, my brother would not have died" (v. 21 NIV).

Beneath their words of pain lurked a lie: *Jesus, You don't care.*

The enemy accuses us all day long before the throne of God (see Revelation 12:10). When God doesn't listen to him, the enemy turns to us and accuses God! I fell for that scheme until Jehovah Mekoddishkem showed Himself to me.

Interestingly, this name is used when God is talking about keeping the Sabbath. When we make time to rest, God makes us holy. The last thing I wanted to do was slow down during my grieving season. It hurt too much. It's what I call God's "violent mercy"—the crucible where faith is forged.

Even when I doubt Him, He's not rattled. He doesn't question His goodness just because I do. He is not threatened by my questions or my anger over His sovereignty. My emotions cannot manipulate Him; instead, He will sanctify me through them. His love remains my anchor, even when I'm too scared or hurt or angry to realize it.

Holy Spirit, teach me to rest. Saturate me in Your holy presence.

JOURNAL

What lies are being exposed in this season of delayed answers and sanctification? What is the truth?

_____

_____

_____

_____

_____

_____

_____

_____

_____

_____

_____

_____

_____

FATHER

DEFENDER

LORI APON, WIDOW

"A father to the fatherless, a defender of widows, is God in his holy dwelling." Psalm 68:5 (NIV)

One Sunday during the service where my husband led worship, Psalm 68:5 was quoted: "A father to the fatherless, a defender of widows ..." I remember thinking how wonderful these truths about God's character were for all those women and children out there who did not have a husband or a father.

By the grace of God, that powerful and life-changing verse declaring God as Defender and Father planted its seed deep within my heart. Less than 24 hours later, a police officer gave me the news that my husband had taken his own life— leaving me a widow with the overwhelming responsibility of raising eight fatherless children.

The enemy came to steal, kill, and destroy. And yet, I had hope. The Holy Spirit had whispered to me the secret to abundant life just hours before God charted my family's next season. He gave me His perspective and taught me to see His character through the lens of Psalm 68:5.

The message I shared with my kids the night of our tragedy has remained our foundation ever since: "Children, you have a new daddy because God promises to be a father to the fatherless."

Knowing God as my Defender and Father to my children brought me to the other side of the valley of the shadow of death.

God *defended me* against the lies of the enemy.

God *fathered my children* through every trial along the way.

His character, as revealed through these names, was undeniable, and His faithfulness to be Defender and Father has never wavered.

JOURNAL

Have you invited your children to see God as a Father? Do you look to God as your Defender? Why or why not?

_____

_____

_____

_____

_____

_____

_____

_____

_____

_____

_____

_____

_____

_____

19

EL KANA
Jealous GOD

DAWN CODRINGTON, PRAYER TEAM

"Do not worship any other god, for the Lord, whose name is Jealous, is a jealous God." Exodus 34:14 (NIV)

Our God is a jealous God. This statement jars us if we think of jealousy in human terms, but it's true.

God doesn't need anything from us. He doesn't compete with anyone. It is not that kind of jealousy.

His jealousy is a passionate, intimate connection with one person that He is not willing to share. This is the heart of El Kana, the God who is jealous for us. He is laser focused on me ... on you. He only has eyes for us and desires the same from us.

Why is this important? For deep, honest intimacy.

I crave intimacy: to be loved with gentleness. Safety. Trust. God offers us a tight bond with Him where we are so in tune that we could finish each other's sentences (see 1 Corinthians 2:16).

We all long for our own love story and romance, and we ache when we can't find it, or when we lose it, or when something gets in the way. Loss hurts. It's agony.

The problem is, deep pain, loneliness, and fear can lead us to look for soothing, numbing, and distraction in every place other than the arms of God. I have found that the "other" ways have led me to more pain, feeling empty and even more disconnected. I have come to see that these idols (things I value and look to before God) always deceive me. I end up taking matters into my own hands and struggling for control.

God is a jealous God. He wants me to love Him first, to trust Him first, and to bring my desperation and desire to Him first. He fights for the purity of our relationship, and it is for my good! Only God can heal my broken heart and provide for my needs. He is the only One. He is my way, my truth and my life.

JOURNAL

Have pain, loneliness, and fear led you to seek comfort in places other than God's arms? He is inviting you to surrender those idols and come to Him today. Will you?

_____

_____

_____

_____

_____

_____

_____

_____

_____

_____

_____

_____

_____

_____

20

JEHOVAH SHALOM
THE LORD MY PEACE

MONICA RICHMOND, PRAYER TEAM

"And He will be the security and stability of your times, a treasure of salvation, wisdom and knowledge; The fear of the LORD is your treasure." Isaiah 33:6 (AMP)

Jehovah Shalom is one of the covenant names by which God has bound Himself to us. Jehovah Shalom brings His wholeness, safety, protection, joy, health, strength, and soundness to our lives.

Jehovah Shalom's presence keeps me in perfect peace amidst the storms of life. Knowing that I can rest in His being pleased with me calms my spirit in the midst of chaos.

When the enemy rages around me, I can stand in the stillness of the promise of Jehovah Shalom. I can stand in complete peace, turning my face toward Him in the center of the storm. Let the storms rage, for I know my God!

Through the revelation of His name, Jehovah Shalom, and the loving peace that comes from the Prince of Peace Himself, I have found security and stability in Him.

Getting to know this beautiful part of His nature has put the pieces of my broken life back together—into the wholeness of His shalom. I am a daughter of Jehovah Shalom!

JOURNAL

Do you know God as a God of peace? Which of Jehovah Shalom's blessings can you testify to in your own life's journey: wholeness, safety, protection, joy, health, strength, and/or soundness?

_____

_____

_____

_____

_____

_____

_____

_____

_____

_____

_____

_____

_____

21

EL ROI
GOD Who Sees

JANA MARSHALL, WIDOW

"If I say, 'Surely the darkness will Hide me and the light become night around me,' Even the darkness will not be dark to you; the night will shine like the day for darkness is as light to you."
Psalm 139:11-12 (NIV)

It was a cool summer night as I sat watching my husband swim his laps in our beautiful community pool. It was our habit to go daily. Bob would swim and I would take in the beauty of the quiet evening.

On this particular night, I could see Bob was struggling to complete his laps. I should not have been surprised, as it was a chemo day. We had been fighting pancreatic cancer for the past year. I was more faith-filled some days than others. But on this particular day, my heart sank as I thought about our struggle. *God, do You even see us?*

Just then, I received a message from a college roommate I hadn't seen in 25 years.

"Jana, I am praying for you," she said.

I quickly responded.

"Thank you! I was just having one of my tear-filled moments. Through your text, God is reminding me He is sovereign and it's okay."

She answered with the words my heart needed.

"God sees you!"

She had no idea I had *just* been wondering about that very thing—but she went on to tell me that the urge to reach out had been too strong to ignore. Only a faithful and all-powerful Father would orchestrate an encounter to remind me that *yes*, He is El Roi, God Who Sees.

I couldn't thank her enough for being sensitive and obedient to what God placed on her heart. And as God would have it, the encouragement went both ways.

God continues to teach me about how He works through the Body of Christ to build up the saints. While humbled to be on the receiving end, it's my prayer to be on the giving end as life moves forward—to be sensitive and obedient to His call! God sees us even in the darkest times of our lives.

JOURNAL

Do you ever wonder if God sees you? Ask El Roi, the God Who Sees, in earnest and see how He chooses to reveal Himself to you.

_____

_____

_____

_____

_____

_____

_____

_____

_____

_____

_____

_____

_____

_____

_____

22

JEHOVAH SHALOM
GOD OF PEACE

COLLEEN SWIFT, PRAYER TEAM

"Peace I leave with you; my peace I give you. I do not give to you as the world gives. Do not let your hearts be troubled and do not be afraid." John 14:27 (NIV)

My first marriage was a bad one. So when I met my next husband after many years of being single, I felt like it was a gift from God. We had a long and happy marriage. That's why it was such a punch in the gut when he died. And yet, my husband's death was when I discovered God as Jehovah Shalom.

I was in shock—traumatized. I vividly remember seeing and feeling a three-inch flame in my gut. I heard the Lord say to me, "You are going to grieve this loss deeply. Know I am with you; My peace I give to you."

When the Lord speaks peace, He creates peace, because the words that He speaks are always spirit and life (see John 6:63). *Shalom* is a Hebrew word meaning peace, harmony, wholeness, completeness, prosperity, tranquility, healing rest, and well-being. This peace He spoke over me.

I had days—even years—of confusion, anger, and misunderstanding with God. And yet, the peace within me would not leave. My prayer almost daily was, "Lord, keep me in perfect cadence with You. I don't want to run ahead of You in my grieving process, and I don't want to lag behind You in it."

Another scripture that was so relevant to me personally during those years was Isaiah 43:1-4. It became so personal, I would speak it aloud over myself, swapping "Jacob" and "Israel" for my own name.

"But now, this is what the Lord says—he who created you, [Colleen], he who formed you, [Colleen]:

'Do not fear, for I have redeemed you; I have summoned you by name; you are mine. When you pass through the waters, I will be with you; and when you pass through the rivers, they will not sweep over you. When you walk through the fire, you will not be burned; the flames will not set you ablaze. For I am the Lord your God, the Holy One of Israel, your Savior'" (NIV, emphasis mine).

Jesus has been a gracious blessing of peace exhibited in and through me. I still carry the flame in me. It is a constant reminder that Jesus is my Jehovah Shalom amongst the chaos of living on this earth. As I have walked in this shalom, I am blessed to be known as someone who carries the peace of God with me everywhere I go.

JOURNAL

Speak Isaiah 43:1-4 over yourself by swapping out the names "Jacob" and "Israel" with your own. How did making this verse personal speak to your heart?

_____

_____

_____

_____

_____

_____

_____

_____

_____

_____

_____

_____

_____

_____

_____

_____

GOD
My Revealer

Karen Booker Schelhaas, Widow

*"When the Red Sea saw you, O God, its waters looked and trembled! The sea quaked to its very depths. The clouds poured down rain; the thunder rumbled in the sky. Your arrows of lightning flashed. Your thunder roared from the whirlwind; the lightning lit up the world! The earth trembled and shook. Your road led through the sea, your pathway through the mighty waters—**a pathway no one knew was there!**" Psalm 77:16-19 (NLT, emphasis mine)*

I have often likened scenes from my widowhood to the children of Israel standing on the shore of the Red Sea with the Egyptian army in hot pursuit. While God helped me move straight through the initial grief of losing my husband and the father of my five children to a rare form of blood cancer in 2019, I had no idea how the secondary losses of an unknown future, pandemic-induced loneliness, and solo-parent exhaustion would leave me standing at a similar dead-end shore.

I have never claimed that the road paved with suffering and loss has been easy or pleasant. In fact, I have come to view lament as a form of worship. But I got to a point where there seemed to be a lack of viable options for true forward motion, and it was really hard to see God in any direction. The fleeing nation of Israel—God's beloved, like me—saw no foreseeable way forward, either. I can only imagine how trapped, ambushed, confused, and fearful they must have felt in those terrifying moments as the dust from the Egyptian chariots rose higher in the sky.

But God.

What we know for sure is that we can't split the sea by ourselves. Our ways pale in comparison to God's ways; He is not just a bigger version of us. "When the Red Sea saw you, O God, its waters looked and trembled!" (Psalm 77:16 NLT). The sea doesn't tremble in our presence. In fact, it often threatens to swallow us up, drowning us whole.

How many of us have stood on the shore, seeing no possible way to redemption—to deep holes being filled, to kids recovering from the loss of their father and then thriving, to lasting provision, to true joy? Calling my family's situation "impossible" seemed justified for a while, especially as I applied my earthly understanding to what appeared to be truly hopeless. That narrative can become a sick torment that is carefully veiled with enough truth to make us believe it *is* the truth.

But God.

In a wild, sky-splitting symphony of natural wonders, the waters unexpectedly pulled back to reveal a hidden way through. "Your road led through the sea, your pathway through the mighty waters—*a pathway no one knew was there!*" (Psalm 77:19 NLT, emphasis mine)

It takes a minute to move when you're dumbfounded. I often stumble around a bit before I get going, especially without my lifelong partner by my side. Hidden pathways can be scary at first, and new roads of possibility begin at such seemingly impossible starting gates sometimes. But I have walked through more than one of them since being widowed, and God is helping me blaze new trails toward my future.

These walks are rife with pure wonder, and I am learning never to underestimate the mighty wake behind Jesus. The surprising walls of water around me "hem me in, behind and before" (Psalm 139:5 NIV), assuring me of His faithful presence. In front of me lies an altered version of a meaningful life that God is working with me to embrace. As I walk, I am steadied by the firm grip of my solid, unwavering Jesus; He never tires as I stumble and stride. And drowning somewhere behind us are the taunts of fear and doubt doing their best to resist their watery demise.

But God.

The redemption of my difficult story may never be falling in love with a new partner, finding a meaningful job outside of my home, watching my kids succeed, or entering some kind of promised land on Earth. I will certainly celebrate those things if and when they happen. But the real redemption of my story is in knowing and believing with all of my heart that no matter how rocky the path, how high the walls of water, or how impossible the way forward may look, my God will make a way for me and my kids.

He is *with* us. And He makes ways where there simply are none; I spot these hidden pathways with greater vision now. I am learning to anticipate them as I baby-step my way forward, keeping my eyes wide open and trusting for what I cannot yet see. Last I checked, that's a pretty good definition of faith.

JOURNAL

What hidden pathways have you encountered on your journey? Write down at least one small way that God has made a way for you.

_____

_____

_____

_____

_____

_____

_____

_____

_____

_____

_____

_____

_____

_____

24

JEHOVAH 'ORI
The LORD My Light

Kaylan Lewis, Widow Daughter

*"The LORD [Jehovah] is my Light ['Ori] and my salvation;
whom shall I fear?" Psalm 27:1 (NIV)*

When I was a little girl, I was deeply afraid of the dark.
It's one of the earliest memories I have of feeling
anxious.

I can still feel in my bones the worry that would build up
as the lights went out at night. It was a sinking feeling, as if
someone had thrown the heaviest weighted blanket over my
head, but my arms would not allow me to pull it off. I would
lie under my sheets staring at the ceiling, frozen, thinking if I
did not find a way to unfreeze myself, I might not find a way
out of the worry and fear.

The anxiety continued to enter my consciousness night after night. Until one day, I was gifted the most beautiful handmade blown-glass nightlight. The glass formed a little girl in a dark pink nightgown on her knees, eyes closed, hands together praying—and all around her was a warm glow.

The first time I saw it, I remember thinking, *Oh! That's ... me!*

It was the most perfect reminder that while the nightlight itself was giving off the tiniest light in a dark room, I was also surrounded by the Lord (Jehovah) My Light ('Ori) who will never leave me alone in the darkness.

Now as an adult, and a mama myself, I have to admit I am still quite fearful of the dark. Sometimes that darkness is the actual dark of the night, but many times it is the darkness of anxiety, loss, unworthiness, or loneliness.

While I cannot carry that precious nightlight with me anymore, I do carry all that it represents with me in my heart. I can close my eyes and say to myself, *Jehovah 'Ori, I am not alone. You are my light. Wherever I go, I know Your light will lead me.*

In John 8:12, Jesus says, "I am the light of the world. Whoever follows me will have the light of life and will never walk in darkness" (ESV).

When those moments creep back in throughout your life, say to yourself, *Jehovah 'Ori, I am not alone. You are my light. Wherever I go I know Your light will lead me.*

Let those words wrap you up like a warm blanket. Not like the weighted one I mentioned before, but instead a warm, quilted one that's like a hug straight from God.

Remember, God will be your light wherever you go today. When the light looks like it has gone out, repeat the words again and allow your body and mind to be at peace. He promises He will be your light always.

JOURNAL

How is God shining light in dark places in your life right now? Where do you still need Him to shine His light?

_____

_____

_____

_____

_____

_____

_____

_____

_____

_____

_____

_____

_____

JEHOVAH NISSI
GOD My Banner

Julie Keeter, Widow

"And Moses built an altar, and called the name of it Jehovah-nissi." Exodus 17:15 (ASV)

Recently, I came across a Bible that my big sister and brother-in-law gave me on my 18th birthday in 1975. They had both recently accepted Jesus as Lord and Savior and were eager to sharethe truth with me. Tucked inside the pages was a photo of me being baptized three years later.

Finding the Bible and seeing the photo stirred up such emotion inside me. As I began to think back over the course of my life since my baptism in 1978, there was much I wanted to say to that young girl.

First, I would tell her that she was more than enough.

Second, that she was loved beyond reason and worthy of that love.

Finally, I would tell her to hold tight to the Lord…for she had no idea the life she was about to walk into.

As I reflect on that day now, I realize how many times God has been Jehovah Nissi to me. His banner over me has always been love. It is the lullaby He sings to me in times of sorrow and pain, and the same song He sings over me on the mountaintop.

God's glorious banner waves over us as a reminder that He is here. He always has been, and He will forever lead us to victory.

Help me to see and trust in You today, Lord God, my Jehovah Nissi, as I lift my hands high and proclaim Your banner of love and victory over my life.

JOURNAL

If the Lord's banner over you is love, how does that shape your identity in times of sorrow and pain as well as mountaintop moments of joy?

_____

_____

_____

_____

_____

_____

_____

_____

_____

_____

_____

_____

_____

𝒬6

JEHOVAH RAPHA
THE LORD WHO HEALS

KRISTY CHANCY, WIDOW

"The thief comes only to steal and kill and destroy. I have come that they may have life, and have it to the full." John 10:10 (NIV)

Shortly after the traumatic passing of my husband, Richard, in November 2019, my daughter, Jordan, and I began finding his journals scattered all around our house. My husband loved journaling. It was his way of walking and talking daily with God, and each one became such a gift to my daughter and me.

I can't tell you how much I have loved having this piece of him—reading his deepest thoughts and seeing how he brought all of them to the Lord in anticipation of their rich conversations. Richard would write his own thoughts in black ink, and what he heard God say in response was written in red. I'm so grateful he had that kind of intimacy with our heavenly Father.

While in our basement one morning, Jordan came across another journal—but this one took on new meaning. After thumbing through it, she stumbled upon a random entry smack dab in the middle that read, *"Kristy, if you are reading this—I love you. If something has happened to me, know that I was ready and that if I'm gone, only now am I FULLY AWAKE. I love you and Jordan, and I'll see you soon."*

I literally fell to my knees. That entry was dated over ten years prior to the day he passed. He'd never once mentioned it. There was a side of me that felt peace and comfort in knowing that Richard was fully prepared to meet the Lord when he was called home. But to be honest, I was *not!* I was incredibly angry at God for allowing us to experience such trauma and loss, to be forced to live a life without our favorite person here on Earth.

Because I had already experienced an incredible amount of loss through the sudden passing of both of my parents and five miscarriages, I wrestled with God for quite some time, regularly asking Him, *When is enough enough?* I threw God every "why him," "why me," and "why us" I could think of, which I know He welcomes and can certainly handle.

Months into my grief journey, a dear friend asked me a powerful question.

"Kristy, are you just living not to die?"

Through that conversation, God started opening my eyes. He revealed that I had been living in crippling fear of what would be taken next, and my life had become strictly about surviving. No joy, no peace, certainly not living fully awake. Instead, my daily goal was to simply *not die*.

In John 10:10, Jesus says it plainly: "The thief comes only to steal and kill and destroy; I have come that they may have life, and have it to the full" (NIV). Not life to the full only when in heaven, but life to the full here and now, healed and whole. Because of the Holy Spirit that lives inside of me, I no longer have to allow the enemy control over my thought life. I can live *fully awake*, even in the midst of pain and loss. *Fully awake* to the many ways the Lord has loved me over the past year through community, through conversation, through acts of kindness, through serving others on their grief journey, and through His living Word.

Luke 9:32 says that when Peter and his sleepy companions became *fully awake*, they saw the Lord's glory. Lord, let me wake to see Your glory in all things, in all seasons. Let me live life to the full with confidence that death will not have the last word. I know that's what Richard would want, for me and for Jordan. I know it's what You, Jehovah Rapha, want for us too. Lord, let it be!

JOURNAL

Are you living fully awake, fully prepared to step into the abundant life Jesus died for you to have? Are you ready to experience the glory of God on display?

_____

_____

_____

_____

_____

_____

_____

_____

_____

_____

_____

_____

JEHOVAH TSABA
GOD OUR WARRIOR

MATTIE SELECMAN, WIDOW

"All those gathered here will know that it is not by sword or spear that the LORD saves; for the battle is the LORD's, and he will give all of you into our hands." 1 Samuel 17:47 (NIV)

Every day of my husband's twelve in the ICU felt like war. Each morning I'd wake, dress, and stare into the bathroom mirror, thinking, *I can't quit fighting.* Walking into that hospital felt like walking onto a battlefield with prayer as my only weapon. Little did I know, the battle was just beginning.

Now three years past his death, every day without him continues to be a battle. Sometimes I'm fighting exhaustion. Sometimes fear. Sometimes anger. Sometimes I'm fighting for hope, for a future. Every day, every year may look different, but the path of widowhood feels like war—a mental, emotional, physical, and spiritual war without end.

But what if I told you, it's a war that's *already* been won? What if I told you that the thing that you fear most about your life right now isn't up to you to overcome? What if I told you, "in all these things we are more than conquerors through him who loved us" (Romans 8:37 NIV)?

I remember reading that passage and exhaling as if a thousand-pound weight had been lifted off my grieving shoulders. In a sweet whisper from the Holy Spirit, I was reminded that Jesus doesn't expect me to win my own battles. He's not disappointed that I can't handle the sorrow and struggles of grief on my own. He's not surprised that I'm lying in the middle of the battlefield weeping. I am more than the conqueror of my own story because Jesus has already conquered my sin and sorrow on the cross, once and for all.

As we battle each day, each season of life after loss, we have the ultimate warrior, Jehovah Tsaba, fighting for us. I think of Gideon, the young man whom God called to fight a massive army with just 300 men. I think of David, a teenager who defeated a barbaric giant with a slingshot. I think of Joshua, who took down the towering walls of Jericho with nothing but prayers and trumpets. None of these men had what they needed to win the impossible battles before them. But they surrendered and submitted and called out to Jehovah Tsaba, God Our Warrior, whose power and sovereignty are the only weapons we need.

The fight against sorrow and despair is impossible to win on your own. But you have access to the ultimate warrior, the eternal conqueror, Jesus Christ. Call on Him for the strength, endurance, hope, faith, and trust you need. Hand over your battles to Him and stand in awe of the mighty victories He will work in your life.

JOURNAL

What battles are you fighting right now? Be specific. Will you let Jehovah Tsaba fight for you in this season?

_____

_____

_____

_____

_____

_____

_____

_____

_____

_____

_____

_____

_____

GRACE
GOD of All Grace

KAYLA STOECKLEIN, WIDOW

"And the God of all grace, who called you to his eternal glory in Christ, after you have suffered a little while, will himself restore you and make you strong, firm and steadfast." 1 Peter 5:10 (NIV)

I sank into her couch and fell apart. Her office was a healing place, a sacred space of feeling known, accepted, seen, heard, and loved. Each time I would visit, everything that had been building up inside would rush to the surface. Thoughts, feelings, emotions, wins, losses, frustrations, and fears—they would all come pouring out.

Through tissues and tears, I whispered, "Is this normal? When do I start taking medication for this? Everything feels *so* hard. I am over it; I didn't sign up for this."

With tears of her own, she leaned in close, "Kayla, *it's okay.* You've been through so much this year."

It's okay. It was all I needed to hear. Choosing every single day to continue living after losing my husband to suicide has taken all that I have. Truth is, I'm sad, I'm mad, I'm tired, I'm lost, I'm confused, I'm lonely, and I'm numb—all in the same breath.

But in that moment, I was gently reminded that *it's okay.* I don't have to try to hide it, or fake it, or push it away. There is no right or wrong way to be here. To be here is to be human. And to be human is to experience it all—the ups and downs, the ebbs and flows, the highs and lows, and the scattered in-between. It's all part of life, this wildly broken and beautiful life, and *it's all okay.*

To feel is to be alive, and to be alive is a gift. A gift we take for granted until we lose a life we love. Loss reminds us that life is fleeting, a reminder we need from time to time. The feelings we feel now will end one day, and our end will be the beginning of a new life somewhere else, somewhere far better than this.

For this short time now, we can take a deep breath, and whisper to ourselves that *it's okay.*

If in our anger, we yell … *it's okay.*
If in our heartache, we cry … *it's okay.*
If in our grief, we numb out … *it's okay.*
If in our exhaustion, we rest … *it's okay.*
If in our loneliness, we wallow … *it's okay.*
If in our brokenness, we make mistakes … *it's okay.*

When we whisper *it's okay*, we replace shame with grace—and grace is the best gift we could ever give ourselves. Grace to be real with how we feel, all of the time. Without grace, we will spend our one life always wishing things were different and we will forget it's all a gift. Every single memory, every single day, every single moment, every single breath—a beautiful, precious gift.

In the New Testament, Peter called Him "the God of all grace" (1 Peter 5:10). *All grace!* That means He has an inexhaustible supply of good gifts, which are adequate for every conceivable need, every failure, everything! These gifts of grace are available to all who will receive them, regardless of their performance.

We are alive, we are human, we have feelings, and *it's perfectly okay.*

We are in this thing together, beautiful friend. You are not alone and grace flows like a river from the heart of God to you. He is the God of All Grace.

JOURNAL

What areas of your grief journey are in need of God's grace? What do you need to extend grace and forgiveness to yourself for by saying "it's okay"?

_____

_____

_____

_____

_____

_____

_____

_____

_____

_____

_____

_____

_____

_____

_____

_____

JEHOVAH SHAMMAH
THE LORD IS THERE

MOLLIANNE ELLIOTT, PRAYER TEAM

"But God still loved us with such great love. He is so rich in compassion and mercy. Even when we were dead and doomed in our many sins, he united us into the very life of Christ and saved us by his wonderful grace! He raised us up with Christ the exalted One, and we ascended with him into the glorious perfection and authority of the heavenly realm, for we are now co-seated as one with Christ!" Ephesians 2:4-6 (TPT)

Whoa. Did you catch that last line? Take a closer look.

"[W]e *ascended* [past tense] with Him into the glorious perfection and authority of the heavenly realm, for we are now *co-seated* [present tense] as one with Christ! (emphasis added)"

Those past- and present-tense truths changed everything about my prayer life.

For years, I came to God with a list of "asks," things I needed or things that others needed. I matched verses with every prayer to make sure I got it right. I read books on prayer, recited other people's prayers, and tried new positions like praying on my knees. I even tried cataloging the things I prayed for so I could write in the dates when God answered those prayers. While there is nothing inherently wrong with any of these methods, they just weren't working for me.

Whenever I talked to God, I was never quite sure that what or how I prayed was right or effective. My prayer life felt empty—like I was a lowly intern with a list of requests for a powerful CEO. I didn't realize that God, in the personalities of the Trinity—Father, Son, and Spirit—wanted to talk to me, too! I had heard that His sheep know His voice (see John 10:27), but I didn't yet understand the practicalities of that truth.

As God's daughters, we know His voice even though we might not recognize it at first. Seeing, hearing, sensing, and knowing are just a handful of the ways we can experience God.

Even as I write this, I can hear God's invitation to you—one that might make you let go of your pressing prayer list for a bit and practice the presence with Him.

Come. Sit with Me. Let Me tell you great and mighty things you do not know.

Take a moment and sit with Him in the heavenlies. Give the eyes of your heart (and all your other spiritual senses) permission to experience what it's like to be in your "seat" with Christ.

As you do, here are a few questions you might ask:

What does my seat look like?
How do I feel sitting here?
Jesus, what do You want me to notice?

Then, practice the presence by not just looking and listening for God but also *interacting* with Him—because you know He is Jehovah Shammah, which means "The Lord Is There." Ask, listen, and receive.

Is there anything I need to let go of, Lord? If so, let it go.
Is there anything You want to give me, Lord? If so, receive it.
Is there anything You want to tell me, Lord? Listen and take it in.

No detail is too small. Nothing is random. If you don't understand what you see and hear, simply ask Him for clarity. *What do You want me to know about that?*

One thing is certain: Papa has authority that He is inviting you to walk in. And when you realize that you are co-seated as one with Christ, you realize the truth, you already have access to everything you need, here and now, as part of your Kingdom inheritance. You're a co-heir with Jesus, seated in heavenly realms—and Jehovah Shammah is there.

JOURNAL

Spend a few moments today experiencing your "seat" with Christ in your mind's eye. Write down anything that comes to mind during this experience.

_____

_____

_____

_____

_____

_____

_____

_____

_____

_____

_____

_____

_____

_____

_____

_____

30

ADONAI 'ORI
THE LORD MY LIGHT

KELLI CAMPBELL GOODNOW,
GOLD STAR MILITARY WIDOW

"The Lord is my light and my salvation; whom shall I fear? The Lord is the stronghold of my life, of whom shall I be afraid?" Psalm 27:1 (ESV)

Adonai 'Ori, which means "The Lord My Light," is found only in Psalm 27. Adonai 'Ori is not a comparison. God is not like light; He is light. He is my light.

On January 14, 2016, I went to sleep secure in my marriage, my home, my routines, and my future.

But on January 15, 2016, I woke up to find it all gone, lost to the sea when my husband Shawn's Marine Corps helicopter collided with another off the North Shore of Oahu in the middle of the dark night.

I remember the numbing shock that set in as the sun rose on my new life that morning. I remember sitting on the ground outside my front door trying to reach someone by phone, trying to make my body do something, and trying to make sense of the confusion. I remember the rays of light shining over the velvet green Ko'Olau mountains.

Four wide-eyed children were watching me, questioning me, and I had nothing to give them. I walked back into the house and saw my Bible sitting on the coffee table. So I sat down, picked it up, let it fall open to the middle, and stared at the blur of black and white. I have no idea what Psalm I read that morning, or if I even read it at all. I just knew in that moment we had no other comfort.

And there was peace.

Eventually the officers came to the door and we waited for news from the boats and planes frantically searching the ocean. Friends arrived. Someone fed my children. I sat. I waited. I answered text messages and spoke to my family thousands of miles away on the mainland. They had been the first to hear. The crash was national news long before the sun rose over our faraway little island.

My dad called at 4 a.m. wanting to make sure that my husband was home. I know now that he was. He was Home.

Job said it best in his final chapter: "My ears had heard of you but now my eyes have seen you" (Job 32:5 NIV). In the days and weeks following Shawn's accident, I saw the presence of God in my home and among my friends and family. My future had gone dark, simply disappeared, and it felt like I was frozen in time while everyone and everything around me continued to move forward.

All I could do was the very next thing in front of me: hug a child, walk into the next room, answer the question, attend the military brief, breathe. But as I sat still, watching the world spin around me, it was as if I suddenly saw with fresh eyes the workings of the Lord in our midst.

He provided everything from groceries to folded laundry to finances to next-step answers. Because I couldn't think past the moment, I simply surrendered to His plan for the next. It became clear that He had gone before us. He wasn't surprised by our tragedy as we were, but He had been laying out the path forward from the beginning of time. One decision at a time, He provided the answer. One step at a time, I began climbing a mountain.

I felt His presence physically with us in those early days. I remember trying hard to describe it to someone because it was so real and profound. Holding up my cupped hands, I said I felt like I was broken into a million pieces, but I also felt completely held. Every fragment of my life was cradled in the palm of His hand. I always believed God cared for me and would provide for my family, but in that moment of shattering grief, I actually *felt it*. I knew in the depths of my soul we were going to be okay. I just didn't know how.

When I couldn't see forward and I no longer had plans or answers, I felt like a child again, walking through a sweltering parking lot in the heat of a Texas summer. I have memories of holding my dad's hand with my head down, squinting against the blinding sunshine, watching his feet for each step. As a thirty-six-year-old new widow carrying four little lives into an unknown future, I knew God's light was shining ahead of us—even if I could only see the very next step before me.

My future wasn't dark; it was so blindingly bright my eyes couldn't take it in. But I could see my Father holding my hand. It's a mercy that God doesn't tell us the entire story and an even greater mercy that He does tell us how it ends.

Still, I was afraid. In the moments when I let my mind wander down paths of what-if and what-now, when I had to sign papers and make decisions, when I thought about my beloved's body still missing at sea, I was afraid. When my babies needed comfort, I was afraid I couldn't help them. When they asked for memories and stories, I was afraid of forgetting. When I thought about their futures, I was afraid of my ability to provide or protect. Fear kept me from eating or sleeping; it left me numb.

But God saw my fear. He saw me, and with gentle loving compassion He whispered to me Isaiah 41:13: "For I am the Lord your God who takes hold of your right hand and says to you, Do not fear; I will help you" (NIV).

That scripture reference is now tattooed on my right hand because I wanted to never forget His very real and present help in trouble. I knew one day my desperate moment-by-moment need could be forgotten. No matter the season, whether in the valley or on the mountaintop, He is and will always be my only help and hope. I want to remain surrendered, content to live just one step at a time because I have seen what He will do!

Isaiah 60 holds a parallel verse to Psalm 27: "Arise, shine, for your light has come" (v. 60 NIV). Just after arriving in Kansas City where my children and I would make our way into our new life, I jotted down a note next to verses 19 and 20, which read, "The sun will no more be your light by day, nor will the brightness of the moon shine on you, for the Lord will be your everlasting light, and your God will be your glory. Your sun will never set again, and your moon will wane no more; the Lord will be your everlasting light, and your days of sorrow will end" (NIV).

The note I left for myself there in the margin reads, "It will not always be like this."

I remember the day I stood outside my first new home as a widow, watching a group of men and women from my new church trimming trees, dumping mulch into flower beds, and digging out the stump of an overgrown holly bush. When someone suggested we trim the hedges down to the ground and let them begin anew, I didn't hesitate to make the first cut.

One truckload of trimmings later, there was nothing left save a few leaves poking out of the freshly turned earth like tiny green promises. I planted a host of color to cheer them on—impatiens, petunias, pansies, lilies—and just a handful of days later, they began to show signs of rejoicing. With the weight of gnarled old branches and tangled vines gone, fresh spring green shoots were reaching up and out toward the oak-dappled sun. I stood over them with a watering hose or sat by them on the front porch, watching kids swing on the disc their grandad had hung from a sturdy red oak branch and imagining all the ways I would improve the garden in the coming years. I felt a bit of a silly kinship with those baby hedges. Or maybe not so silly.

They had been cut down but not destroyed. They were surrounded by hope. They were seeking the light, drinking the water. And something new was growing out of those deep and long-established roots.

"I remain confident of this: I will see the goodness of the Lord in the land of the living" (Psalm 27:13 NIV). My friend Christy often sent me this verse in the months and years after my husband's death. It was her constant and faithful prayer over me. The Spirit seemed to always prompt her to remind me just when I needed it most. There are days when my faith feels small and weak. Days when I cannot see past the loneliness and exhaustion of this moment. Days when sorrow rests so heavy over my heart, I can barely breathe.

There was one day, Wednesday, August 9, 2017, to be exact, when I was feeling especially worn down. Emotionally spent, lonely, and weary, I had just gone through a minor basement flood that turned into a major basement cleanout. Mice had overtaken the space, destroying old clothing, blankets, and some toys. Water had seeped into boxes of books and papers.

Unlike most moves where I had sorted and purged and carefully packed away only what was necessary to keep or store, we had packed up quickly to move to Kansas. Shawn's clothes and uniforms were piled up to be sifted through later. There was a box full of items from his dresser, like loose change and old chewing gum. Another box held his shoes—including the pair of Asics he wore on his last run. They still had grass from our backyard on them. I remember clearly that drizzly day he had walked in across the yard wet with rain to take off his shoes at the door, stuffing his sweaty socks inside them.

After the crash, we probably had hundreds of people come through our house, but no one touched or moved those shoes. I remember walking past them so many times, unable to move them. They were comforting in a way, something of him left behind. And they were incredibly sad, something I would have to eventually pick up and put away, something he would never use again.

I don't know who finally had to move the shoes. Maybe it was me. All I know is that when I found them in that box, still grassy and still holding the balled-up socks that once frustrated me as I would have to peel them apart for the laundry, I was transported right back to my doorway in Hawaii. I could see my backyard with the mango and plumeria trees, the kids' pet bunnies, the strings of Edison bulbs, and Shawn. I could see him coming home from work and coming in from a run. I could see him pacing in and out of the house as he reviewed briefs and emergency procedures from his stack of white notecards. I saw him chasing half-naked children out the door to the beach down the street and dusting off their sandy bodies on the way back in after.

When I held Shawn's shoes, I had to instantly face so much loss all over again. I was holding an unbearable weight and felt I would never find my way out from under it. That day, not knowing what I was going through, Christy again sent me the words of Psalm 27:13: "I remain confident of this: I will see the goodness of the Lord in the land of the living." I read the words but didn't really stop to ponder them. I appreciated them but I was also feeling like I'd rather continue in my pity party. I was angry over the basement mess and the unwelcome bombardment of memories. I was sad. I was spent in every way.

Later that same day, my brother-in-law, Brian (M.), shared in a family message thread that he had been listening to one of my favorite artists. This was his message:

"Heard a song called 'Rise' on my Josh Garrels Pandora station this evening based on this verse: 'I remain confident of this: I will see the goodness of the Lord in the land of the living.'"

Same day. Same words. Two different loved ones, one in Japan and one in Texas, while I sat there crushed by grief in Kansas. The Lord certainly had my attention.

Hope is so very real. Just as I had been given a new vision of God, I was given a new understanding of hope. When I had nothing, when every part of my life and my children's lives had been changed or lost, my God remained. My salvation remained. My future in heaven remained and became that much more real knowing how quickly and easily Shawn had slipped through the veil. My need for plans and answers and certainties was stripped away until I knew that the only thing I truly needed, I held in my heart.

When the blurred psalms in my lap were my only comfort, when my heart was broken wide open by grief, when everything material around me suddenly held no eternal value—I was filled. I wasn't restored, but I knew I was *being* restored. I couldn't see past this moment into the next step, but I could see the light peeking over the mountain even as I climbed.

At the end of our first year of sorrow, I decided to send out a Christmas card to the community of friends and family that had been God's hands and feet to us. They had surrounded and held and carried us and I desperately wanted to say, *Thank you. I see Jesus in you. Your love has made all the difference.*

So it was John 1:5 scripted above a photo of Shawn's empty combat boots: "The Light shines in the darkness, and the darkness has not overcome it" (NIV).

That was my heart's message that Christmas, and it is my heart's message to you now. We are broken and hurting still, but we have this hope that will never be taken away. Shawn's shoes and boots remain empty, but the void left in our lives has been a place for the light to shine.

I have a little painting hanging in my office—abstract splashes of color laced together with shiny gold leaf. It represents the idea behind Japanese kintsugi, an art form where broken pottery is sealed back together with precious metals. Rather than hide the breaks, they are made to shine, and the restored piece is more valuable because of its scars. Its history makes it beautiful. I bought the painting because it reminded me of my family—all in pieces but being stitched together by God into something new. His goodness shines in the darkness. It shines brighter because of the darkness.

"...the Lord will be your everlasting light, and your days of sorrow will end" (Isaiah 60:20 NIV).

It will not always be like this. Our Adonai 'Ori has come.

JOURNAL

In what ways has God's goodness been a source of light and life to you in your time of grief?

_____

_____

_____

_____

_____

_____

_____

_____

_____

_____

_____

_____

_____

Never Alone Widows is the outreach arm of **Be Still Ministries** in Atlanta, GA. We exist to love the widow well through weekend encounters, national gatherings, and online resources. Retreats began in 2018 with a simple idea to gather widows together to provide community and comfort. After those first 20 women left transformed, our volunteer team knew what we did was uniquely special. We've been filling the need for more widows to gather, heal, and be loved well ever since.

Since 2014, we have reached thousands of women, ministered to more than 500 widows, and brought freedom to countless families and communities by sharing the goodness of God. We currently offer three-day encounters and national gatherings across the country, and the ministry is working to become the largest Christian widows ministry in the nation.

BE: INSPIRED

Karen Mcadams and Rachel Faulkner Brown host a podcast that inspires women to believe that with God there is always more.

BE: TOGETHER

Quarterly gathering to worship, encourage community, to share life-changing stories, and be empowered through prayer.

BE: EQUIPPED

Discovering biblical truths that create transformation and freedom through Christ-centered curriculum and discipleship.

BE: LOVED

Loving the widow well through weekend encounters, national gatherings, and online resources.

@neveralonewidows

www.neveralonewidows.com

@bestillministries

www.bestillministries.net

Additional Resources

Father's House is an 8-week video-driven Bible study encounter to help you unlock the power of the Father's love for you.

Go-to Girls is a mentoring journey to up-level your living as a daughter through video teaching, community, and digital resources.

He Speaks is a 4-week Bible study curriculum designed to amplify and educate women in their ability to hear God's voice.

FOOTNOTES

1. Jill Bolte Taylor, *A Brain Scientist's Personal Journey* (Hodder & Stoughton Ltd., 2008).

2. Bob Sorge, *The Fire of Delayed Answers* (Canadaigua, NY: Oasis House, 1996).